LOVE
AT
CHRISTMAS

Illustrations by Julie Downing

To

. . . .

. . . .

WITH BEST WISHES

FOR A

HAPPY CHRISTMAS

FROM

. . . .

. . . .

. . . .

U*nto us a boy is born!*
King of all creation,
Came he to a world forlorn,
The Lord of every nation.

Cradled in a stall was he
With sleepy cows and asses:
But the very beasts could see
That he all men surpasses.

translated from the German
by Percy Dearmer

Aᴺd there were shepherds
living out in the fields near by,
keeping watch over their flocks at night.
An angel of the Lord appeared to them,
and the glory of the Lord shone around them,
and they were terrified.
But the angel said to them,
'Do not be afraid.
I bring you good news of great joy
that will be for all the people.
Today in the town of David
a Saviour has been born to you;
he is Christ the Lord.
This will be a sign to you:
You will find a baby
wrapped in strips of cloth
and lying in a manger.'

The Gospel of Luke

chapter 2, verses 8-12

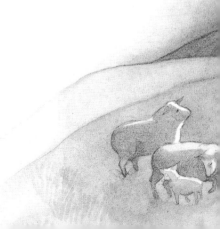

Suddenly a great company of the heavenly host
appeared with the angel, praising God and saying,
'Glory to God in the highest,
and on earth peace
to men on whom his favour rests.'

The Gospel of Luke
chapter 2, verses 13-14

H*ark! the herald angels sing,*
'Glory to the new-born King!
Peace on earth and mercy mild,
God and sinners reconciled.'
Joyful, all ye nations rise —
Join the triumph of the skies;
With th'angelic host proclaim —
'Christ is born in Bethlehem!'
Hark! the herald angels sing,
'Glory to the new-born King!'

Charles Wesley

When the angels had left them
and gone into heaven,
the shepherds said to one another,
'Let's go to Bethlehem
and see this thing that has happened,
which the Lord has told us about.'
So they hurried off
and found Mary and Joseph, and the baby,
who was lying in a manger.
When they had seen him,
they spread the word concerning
what had been told them about this child,
and all who heard it were amazed
at what the shepherds said to them.

But Mary treasured up all these things
and pondered them in her heart.
The shepherds returned,
glorifying and praising God
for all the things they had heard and seen,
which were just as they had been told.

The Gospel of Luke

chapter 2, verses 15-20

Before the world was created,
the Word already existed;
he was with God,
and he was the same as God.
From the very beginning
the Word was with God.

Through him God made all things;
not one thing in all creation
was made without him.
The Word was the source of life,
and this life brought light to mankind.
The light shines in the darkness,
and the darkness has never put it out . . .

The Word became a human being and,
full of grace and truth, lived among us.
We saw his glory,
the glory which he received
as the Father's only Son.

The Gospel of John
chapter 1, verses 1-5,14

O come, all ye faithful,
Joyful and triumphant,
O come ye, O come ye to Bethlehem;
Come and behold him,
Born the King of angels!
 O come, let us adore him,
 O come, let us adore him,
 O come, let us adore him,
 Christ the Lord!

Sing, choirs of angels,
Sing in exultation,
Sing, all ye citizens of heav'n above;
Glory to God in the highest:
   O come, let us adore him,
   O come, let us adore him,
   O come, let us adore him,
   Christ the Lord.

translated from the Latin
by Frederick Oakeley

Illustrations copyright © 1989 Julie Downing
This edition copyright © 1989 Lion Publishing

Published by
Lion Publishing plc
Sandy Lane West, Littlemore, Oxford, England
ISBN 0 7459 1572 8
Lion Publishing Corporation
1705 Hubbard Avenue, Batavia, Illinois 60510, USA
ISBN 0 7459 1572 8
Albatross Books Pty Ltd
PO Box 320, Sutherland, NSW 2232, Australia
ISBN 0 7324 0015 5

First edition 1989

Acknowledgments
Bible quotations from the *Holy Bible*,
New International Version (British edition),
copyright 1978 New York International Bible Society

Printed and bound in Italy